PARENTING WITHOUT REGRET
WORKBOOK

JIMMY & LAURA SEIBERT

C|D
CLEARDAY

PARENTING WITHOUT REGRET WORKBOOK

Copyright © 2018 Jimmy and Laura Seibert.

All rights reserved. No portion of this book may be reproduced, stored in a retrieval system, or transmitted in any form or by any means—electronic, mechanical, photocopy, recording, scanning, or other—except for brief quotations in critical reviews or articles, or as specifically allowed by the U. S. Copyright Act of 1976, as amended, without the prior written permission of the publisher.

Published by Clear Day Publishing, a division of Clear Day Media Group LLC, Waco, TX. cleardaypublishing.com.

Published in association with Lux Creative {theluxcreative.com}

Scripture quotations taken from the New American Standard Bible® (NASB), Copyright © 1960, 1962, 1963, 1968, 1971, 1972, 1973, 1975, 1977, 1995 by The Lockman Foundation. Used by permission. www.Lockman.org

Scripture taken from the HOLY BIBLE, NEW INTERNATIONAL VERSION®. NIV®. Copyright © 1973, 1978, 1984 by International Bible Society. Used by permission of Zondervan. All rights reserved worldwide.

Scripture quotations marked NLT are taken from the Holy Bible, New Living Translation, copyright © 1996, 2004, 2015 by Tyndale House Foundation. Used by permission of Tyndale House Publishers, Inc., Carol Stream, Illinois 60188. All rights reserved.

Scripture quotations marked TPT are from The Passion Translation®. Copyright © 2017, 2018 by Passion & Fire Ministries, Inc. Used by permission. All rights reserved. ThePassionTranslation.com.

ISBN: 978-1-7326252-0-4
Library of Congress Control Number: 2018954780

Cover Design: Carolynn Seibert {carolynnseibert.com}
Interior Design: Lux Creative {theluxcreative.com}

Printed in the United States of America.

HI FRIEND!

I already know that if you took the time to open this workbook, you're really serious about your parenting and ready to work. I wish I could guarantee that if you merely read the pages of *Parenting Without Regret* you would see changes in yourself, your kids, and your family as a whole. But we all know that it's implementation and practice that makes lasting change. Both *PWR* and this workbook are about stirring discussion, offering application, and getting you connected to God to be able to create the family culture you desire.

Our goal is to share concepts and ideas that we used in raising our kids. Let me say, in no way do we think we did it all perfectly, but we have seen fruit and so have those around us. In fact, the book came about because so many people were asking us for advice and telling us we need to write this down for others to know. We pray that the *PWR* book and this workbook create a structure to start a great adventure of becoming the parent you want to be. This book can be used for you personally, as a couple, or in a group setting.

Way to go! Jimmy and I are so proud of you and we want to hear from you. Please take the time to email us as you work through these pages and let us know how it's going.

Father, I ask for Your wisdom to rule and reign on every parent who is reading these pages. Proverbs 8 says that when we look for wisdom we will find it. I ask that each parent that picks up this workbook will be filled with Your wisdom and be given Your insight into the specific plans You have for them. Thank You that You created us in Your image and are crafting a unique story for each of us. We are dependent on Your leadership and direction. We declare You are good and You are for us, and the plans that You have for us, Your kids, is for our good. You are ordering our future and filling us with hope. Our hearts say thank You for what You are going to do. In the mighty name of Jesus. Amen.

Laura Seibert
laura.seibert@antioch.org

> *"May God Himself, the Heavenly Father of our Lord Jesus Christ,*
> *release grace over you and impart total well-being into your lives."*
> **Ephesians 1:2**, *The Passion Translation*

PARENTING WITHOUT REGRET
WORKBOOK

CHAPTER 1
PARENTING FROM WHOLENESS 3

CHAPTER 2
THE VALUE OF OUR CHILDREN 7

CHAPTER 3
YOU ARE THE #1 INFLUENCER 11

CHAPTER 4
PLACING IDENTITY ON THEM 15

CHAPTER 5
PRAYING FOR YOUR KIDS 19

CHAPTER 6
CONNECTING YOUR KIDS TO GOD 23

CHAPTER 7
TEACHING THEM TO FOLLOW JESUS ALONG THE WAY 27

CHAPTER 8
INTENTIONAL PURSUIT 31

CHAPTER 9
FAMILY: FRIENDS FOR LIFE 35

CHAPTER 10
YOUR KIDS AND THEIR FRIENDS 39

CHAPTER 11
THE CHURCH COMMUNITY **43**

CHAPTER 12
ON THE RUN (SCHOOL AND OTHER EXTRA CURRICULAR ACTIVITES) **47**

CHAPTER 13
HELPING THEM TO OVERCOME **51**

CHAPTER 14
TRAINING THEM TO OBEY **55**

CHAPTER 15
PROTECTING PURITY **59**

CHAPTER 16
TEACHING WORK ETHIC **63**

CHAPTER 17
MONEY AND POSSESSIONS **67**

CHAPTER 18
DEFINING MOMENTS **71**

CHAPTER 19
DATING AND ATTRACTION **75**

CHAPTER 20
FOCUSED AND INTENTIONAL **79**

CHAPTER 21
WHERE DO WE GO FROM HERE **83**

CHAPTER 1

PARENTING FROM WHOLENESS

"Search me, O God, and know my heart; test me and know my anxious thoughts. Point out anything in me that offends You, and lead me along the path of everlasting life."
Psalm 139:23-24, *New Living Translation*

Both Jimmy and Laura shared about brokenness in their early years that caused them to develop hurtful habits. Take a moment and ask God to show you any lies you believe about yourself, beliefs that don't line up with who He says you are. Then ask God to show you how He sees you and the things He has put in you that He loves. **Write down what God tells you.**

LIES:

TRUTHS:

Wholeness focuses on the power of RECEIVING forgiveness from God and EXTENDING forgiveness to those who have hurt us. Which do you need to focus on in this season? Ask God to show you how to best focus on this area. (You might need to seek help from a trusted friend, mentor, or counselor.) **Jot down your answers.**

RECEIVING FORGIVENESS:

EXTENDING FORGIVNESS:

LEGACY BUILDING EXERCISE

Jimmy and Laura also talked about three factors that they prioritized in their new home together:
      1. Establishing a biblical worldview
      2. Prioritizing their marriage (each other)
      3. Parenting on the same team

Choose one of these factors to prioritize in your home this week and think of one step you can take to put this factor into practice. (For example, we will focus on number two, so this week we will have a date night.)

CHAPTER
2

THE VALUE OF CHILDREN

In chapter two, Laura shared a moment of epiphany when she realized that she needed to see and value her kids as God does. What about you? **Take a moment to examine your own heart. Describe/Discuss your perspective on the value of children.**

"Children are a gift from the LORD; they are a reward from him. Children born to a young man are like arrows in a warrior's hands. How joyful is the man whose quiver is full of them! He will not be put to shame when he confronts his accusers at the city gates."
Psalm 127:3-5, NLT

After looking at these verses, what does God say about children? Are they a blessing or a burden? **Write your response to these verses in the space below.**

Children are our eternal inheritance. They last **FOREVER**, past our earthly life into eternity. **On a scale of 1 to 10, where would you rate how you value your children and family?**
(Remember, where we spend our time shows our values.)

```
    1_____10
 Burden                                  Blessing
```

Now think about your time and investment in them. **How would you rate that?**

1_____10

Low Investment					High Investment

Describe one practical way you can invest more time in your family this week.

 Pray and ask God for the grace and courage to make the necessary changes.

LEGACY BUILDING EXERCISE

Take time each day this week to communicate to your child their value to you and to God.
Write below what you did.

Monday:
    To you-   To God-

Tuesday:
    To you-   To God-

Wednesday:
    To you-   To God-

Thursday:
    To you-   To God-

Friday:
    To you-   To God-

Saturday:
    To you-   To God-

Sunday:
    To you-   To God-

CHAPTER
3

YOU ARE THE #1 INFLUENCER

It starts with you. "My kids were watching my life. From the way I treated my wife, to the media choices I made, to the way I talked about others, my lifestyle taught them more than words alone ever could." - Jimmy, *PWR* page 33

What aspects of your lifestyle, habits, and mannerisms provide a positive influence on your children? **Write three.**

1.

2.

3.

What aspects of your lifestyle, habits, and mannerisms provide a negative influence on your children? **Write three.**

1.

2.

3.

Pray and ask God to show you how you can be mindful of modeling what you want your kids to value and do.

 "For it is God who works in you to will and to act in order to fulfill His good purpose."
Philippians 2:13, *New International Version*

LEGACY BUILDING EXERCISE

Think about an area of influence where God is prompting growth in you. This week, initiate with someone you have observed to be strong in that area and begin a conversation with them. Communicate your desire to grow and ask them for counsel on ways to develop your character in that area.

What area?

I will initiate a conversation with

This chapter brought up three ways parents influence their children (listed below). **Circle the area in which you'd like to grow. Then list 3 ways you can practically do this.**

BY THEIR WORDS	BY THEIR LIFESTYLE	BY THEIR PRESENCE

1.

2.

3.

CHAPTER
4

PLACING IDENTITY ON THEM

This chapter is about placing identity on your children. **To do this with confidence we must see our kids as God sees them.** List your children's names. Write some thoughts about what you see in their personalities and character.

Based on the thoughts you wrote, are you seeing the negative or the positive in them?

Read Isaiah 49:16 and write it below.

We are always on God's mind. We are so special that our names are written on the palms of His hands. If you are seeing only the negative in your children (don't worry, you are not alone), then revelation is still needed to see them as God sees them.

 Pray and ask God to give you His thoughts about each of your children.

LEGACY BUILDING EXERCISE

Sometimes we need help seeing our children as God sees them. Take time this week to write your child's name on an index card and ask God to show you what He says about them.

Then find a Scripture to back up what God says about your child and write in on the card. Place the card on your bathroom mirror and pray it over your child as you get ready each morning.

CHAPTER
5

PRAYING FOR YOUR KIDS

Chapter five starts with a quote from the parable of the persistent widow who prayed in desperation. The beginning of this story says:

"He was telling them a parable to show that at all times they ought to pray and not to lose heart."
Luke 18:1, New American Standard Bible

Where are you losing heart with your child? Note that in the space below and honestly tell God you are losing heart, and with fresh faith, ask for His help in this area for your child's life.

On page 56 Jimmy says, "Laura and I are motivated to pray because we recognize our own limitations."
Take a moment to reflect on that. What does that mean to you?

No parent is perfect. That is why we need a Savior and the Holy Spirit to lead us. Our best investment is to pray for our children and for His will and His purposes to be accomplished in their lives. *In our weakness we pray for God to take up our lack.* Prayer is the partnership in which we release our kids into His hands and ask Him to move in their lives.

So where do we start? **Pray and ask God for a biblical promise for each of your kids and write it below.**

Child 1:

Child 2:

Child 3:

Child 4:

LEGACY BUILDING EXERCISE

Take the biblical promise you wrote down and begin praying it daily over each of your children. We suggest that if your children are little, you can tell them what you are praying and pray it aloud as they go to sleep.

Example: We have often told our younger kids how kindness and truth are beneficial to them and to their success: "Do not let kindness and truth leave you; bind them around your neck, and write them on the tablet of your heart" *Proverbs 3:3, NASB*

If you have teenagers, depending where you are in this journey, you can share with them what you are praying and believing for them. If that step feels too vulnerable then keep those prayers before God, but we do recommend you go into their room during the day when they are gone and pray these over them. As our children grew older, we often reminded them of these specific promises.

Example: One of the many scriptures we have prayed over our older kids is "The hand of the diligent will rule, but the slack hand will be put to forced labor." *Proverbs 12:24, NASB*. We believe that if our kids have a strong work ethic they will find themselves in a place of influence and leadership.

CHAPTER
6

CONNECTING YOUR KIDS TO GOD

Fill in the blanks using Psalm 34:8:
"_____and see that the Lord is_____;
blessed is the one who takes refuge in Him." NIV

We love this passage. It motivated us to encourage our children to connect with God personally because only the Holy Spirit can create a hunger for God.

Take time to reflect on how much you personally make connecting with God a priority. Jot down your thoughts.

We'd suggest letting your kids see your genuine desire to connect with God every day: through reading your Bible during your quiet time, playing worship music, or singing along to Christian songs as you do things around the house. When you get in the car, share with them one of your new favorite worship songs or ask them what theirs is and listen to it together.

How do you best connect with God in a life-giving way? (For example, walking in nature, drinking coffee while reading your Bible in the early morning, worshiping and praying in the car as you drive, etc.)

Now, ask your kids that question. Find out how they are wired and give them opportunities in these areas! (Pages 70-73 in the *PWR* book can give you some creative ideas if needed.)

LEGACY BUILDING EXERCISE

In keeping with your family's season, brainstorm several ways you can make connecting with God together a priority. For example, if your kids are toddlers, we suggest starting your morning with a family devotional (it can be as simple as the five-minute JellyTelly devotion). If they are elementary age, try acting out Bible stories or memorizing scripture to hand motions. For pre-teen or older, we found reading a Proverb a day was a great way to connect with God and start our day as a family. **Remember, our goal is not perfection.** Our goal is to invite the Holy Spirit into everything we do.

Write what you came up with here.

CHAPTER
7

TEACHING THEM TO FOLLOW JESUS ALONG THE WAY

Fill in the blanks using Deuteronomy 6:6-7:
"These words, which I am_____you today, shall be on your heart. You shall_____them diligently to your sons and shall talk of them when you_____in your house and when you_____by the way and when you_____and when you_____up."
NASB

This Scripture calls us to make our walk with God an everyday, every moment experience.
What is one way you can implement this advice into your daily routine with your children?

On page 78, Laura talked about losing vision and having her priorities out of whack. Having a family mission is one of the ways that has helped keep priorities aligned. For years, it was posted on the wall near our table. It read, "We are a family of love, honor, and purpose," and included a Scripture underneath each of the words.

LEGACY BUILDING EXERCISE

Think about your family. **In the space below, write out a mission statement.** Make it simple and doable. Post it somewhere in your house, explain to your kids what it means, and memorize it together.

OUR FAMILY MISSION STATEMENT:

Now do something this week that fleshes out the mission (for example, write an encouraging note, make cookies and deliver them, invite someone to church, etc.)

One way our family fleshed out love and honor was to reach out to someone else. Think of a co-worker, school friend, or family member who needs encouragement. Pray with your child about what you can do to encourage him or her and do it.

What did you do?

CHAPTER
8

INTENTIONAL PURSUIT

We live busy lives, and if you have multiple kids this can feel overwhelming. Take a moment each day to ask God to show you which of your children needs immediate pursuit and the most effective way to meet their needs.

Remember, listening is the easiest and quickest way to connect with your child.

Fill in the blanks using James 1:19:
"Be quick to_____ and slow to_____." NIV

Do you feel like you are a good listener? How would your kids say you are doing with listening? Be brave and ask them!

"Dating" your kids is very important. Is there anything preventing you from making this a priority? Talk to your spouse or friends, check the internet, or ask God for a creative, fun, simple, and cheap way to go on a short date with one of your kids and go do it. *You won't regret it!* **Jot down a few ideas for how you can take your kids on 'dates'.**

LEGACY BUILDING EXERCISE

Question asking is a great skill to develop. This helps your children process what is going on in their world and gives you the chance to connect with them. Think of someone who asks good questions and pick their brain for a bit.

Here are few good questions we have asked:
- What is the highlight of your day?
- What is one thing that happened today that you want me to know about?
- What happened today that is disappointing to you?
- What do you need from me right now (for an older child)?

If you feel connected in this way, take time this week to go to one of your child's events and just sit there and be with them.

CHAPTER
9

FAMILY: FRIENDS FOR LIFE

"A man of too many friends comes to ruin, but there is a friend who sticks closer than a brother."
Proverbs 18:24, *NASB*

This Scripture teaches that the man with the most friends doesn't actually win. Having (and being) a true friend is what matters. A true friend is authentic, servant-hearted, loyal, and faithful to the bone. He challenges others to be all God created them to be. He is always there for others no matter what life holds. Being this kind of person is important in friendships, but even more so in families. Friends come and go, but your family will always be there, influencing and affecting you in one way or another. That's why it's important to be intentional in creating a family culture.

What kind of family culture do you want to have? Think about what your family culture was like growing up. What do you want to add to it and what do you want to change?
Write that down below.

One sure thing is that all families have conflict. It's the nature of relationships. So, in creating a friendly family culture, it's a good idea to have a plan for conflict resolution.

What does conflict resolution look like in your home? How do you feel like it's going? What are some new practices you can begin using this week?

Note: If you find that your family has been having a lot of conflict, we have found that as the parent being the first to repent for the ways you have failed or been stubborn is one of the best ways to create family unity.

There are many ways to make communication a priority and learn to do it well. We mentioned creating a traditional question that was asked at each family meal. If you're past that stage, (high schoolers are hard to get home consistently) use a phone app like GroupMe or Voxer. **Write a traditional question below.**

LEGACY BUILDING EXERCISE

Creating a friendly family culture takes intentionality. There are so many ways you can bring your family together, regardless of your stage of life. Find one thing you can do this week and make it happen. Here are some ideas to help you get started:

- Begin a family fun night and make it a weekly tradition.
- Take a mini-vacation and do something epic. Even if it's close to home and you don't have a lot of money, your time and thought into it are what make it memorable.
- Support each other's activities, events, and interests by having the whole family attend a game or participate if possible.
- Liven up family meals by sitting around the table asking fun questions and actively listening to one another.

How did it go? **Write a description below of your family's experience of coming together this week.**

CHAPTER
10

YOUR KIDS AND THEIR FRIENDS

Fill in the blanks using 1 Corinthians 15:33:
"_____company_____good morals." NIV

Are you aware of who your kids are spending time with? On the bus? At school? The playground? Their sports team? Who are their social media friends? **Write below how you feel about who your kids spend time with. If you realize you need to know more about their friends, make it a point this week to put your new listening and question-asking skills into play.**

What about your values—do your kids know and honor your family values? Are they willing and able to stand firm on them?

Are they strong enough to be influencers or are they the ones being influenced?

 Take time to pray for your kids to be influencers to their peers.

NOTES

LEGACY BUILDING EXERCISE

In *PWR* we talked about having a strategy set in place if your kids want out of a situation. Role play a few scenarios with your older ones to find out what they would do when faced with peer pressure. Give them some suggestions and have a private escape plan if needed. Teach them how to have a voice or a way out.

With younger ones, invite their friends over and spend the day listening. Drop all that you are doing and intentionally listen to their interactions and see if you agree or disagree with what you are hearing. Take the time later in the evening to talk about their interactions that day. Review with them what you heard that was positive and share areas that need growth.

CHAPTER
11

THE CHURCH COMMUNITY

 Fill in the blanks using Proverbs 16:18:
"_____ goes before _____,
a _____ spirit before a fall." NIV

Transparency and teachability are two necessary factors in raising children. Do you have a community of godly people who can speak into your life of parenting? If so, who are they? **Write a few of the names below. If not, prayerfully search for a few who would be willing to partner with you.**

Take a step back and look at yourself. Do people feel like they can speak into your life without you getting defensive? Are you teachable? **Write below a time that you were corrected and how it went.**

LEGACY BUILDING EXERCISE

It's important to keep an open heart and invite people into your parenting process. Initiate with someone this week and invite them to speak into your life regarding your parenting. Ask if there is anything they are concerned about. End your time asking them to pray over you and thank them for their willingness to share with you.

CHAPTER
12

ON THE RUN

Fill in the blanks using Psalm 90:12:
"_____us to_____our days, that we might present to you a heart of wisdom." NASB

We have found that if we do not intentionally pause in every season and evaluate what everyone is doing and seeing if these activities line up with our goals, life will run away with our schedule.

Think about your schedule. We each have only 24 hours in a day and once it's gone, it's gone. Take a moment to stop and ask yourself, *"Does my schedule control me, or do I control my schedule?"* Write your thoughts below.

Does your family have guidelines as to how you will pick what activities you engage in? If not, take some time to think through how you can spend your time wisely.

NOTES

LEGACY BUILDING EXERCISE

Write everyone's name on an index card. Next to each, put down all the activities they are involved in.

Now pull out a calendar and fill in the month. How does it look? Are you happy with the amount of activity that is going on? Is there room for connecting with God and family? If you feel like there needs to be changes, call a family meeting and show everyone the schedule.

Discuss what changes need to be made to keep your priorities of family devotions and family time. Remember you have to have a plan to be in control of your time.

CHAPTER
13

HELPING THEM TO OVERCOME

Write each of your kids' names on a sheet a paper and think of one area in their life that needs extra help and support (physically, academically, socially, or spiritually).

 Read Psalm 84:11 and write it below.

Think about this Scripture. God is withholding nothing from our children. He has a great plan and when we take time to stop and listen He will reveal our part in helping meet their needs. We all want things comfortable for our kids and don't like challenges. We want everything to go their way and for them to be happy. But life is not about comfort, happiness, and avoiding pain at all costs. Life is about finding a close relationship with God and growing in character. This character only comes through facing challenges and learning to overcome them, and one of our roles as parents is to help teach them to do it.

NOTES

LEGACY BUILDING EXERCISE

Find the index card where you filled in what areas of growth you are wanting in your children. Ask the Holy Spirit for one way you can come alongside them and help them grow or overcome in that area.
Write down what He shows you.

Sit down this week with each of your kids and start communicating how you want to help him or her. Then make a plan to help your child take a step toward wholeness. Don't get overwhelmed; just take one step at a time. If you need help with this exercise, call a friend and ask them to share ideas of what they have done, or brainstorm with you to get a plan.

CHAPTER
14

TEACHING THEM TO OBEY

This is the most controversial yet necessary chapter in the book.

We want to emphasize that no matter your training and discipline style, you need to choose one that trains and requires obedience, agree on it, implement it, and stick to it.

The method we shared worked great for us and our kids because it contained clarity, consistency, and restoration.

In our fast-paced culture, we want everything to have fast results. If we do not see change quickly, we can start to question, which leads us to inconsistency, and eventually leads us to quit and try other things. *If your structure is based on love and the Word of God, you can be confident that you will eventually see results!*

Write out these Scriptures:
Proverbs 12:1

Proverbs 5:23

Proverbs 6:23

Proverbs 19:2

The trend today is not only child-centered but child-empowering, pushing small kids to find their voice, exercise their power, and become prematurely independent. Eventually all these ideas are great for older children/adults once they have learned to be obedient to authority and honor the ways of God.

What structure do you have in place for your child to learn obedience? Is it working? Are you consistent? Are you in agreement with your spouse?

LEGACY BUILDING EXERCISE

Talk with your spouse about discipline and training. If you are not in agreement or just need further guidance, call someone you respect who has older kids. Whether you are married or single, set up a time to meet with others and discuss ways you can foster obedience in your children. Below are some more Scriptures on discipline. Take time to study these passages and process them with others.

- Proverbs 22:6

- Proverbs 22:15

- Proverbs 23:13-14

- Proverbs 29:15

- Proverbs 29:17

- Proverbs 29:19

CHAPTER
15

PURITY

Fill in the blanks using:
Psalms 101:3: "I will_____no_____thing before my eyes." NASB

Matthew 5:8: "Blessed are the_____in heart, for they shall_____God." NASB

Proverbs 4:23: "_____ all else, _____ your heart, for everything you do flows from it." NIV

What do you think the Scripture is saying in the verses above?

Particularly for younger children, who do you think is responsible for what your children see?

Are you comfortable with the standards for purity you have set in your own personal life and in your home? What would you change?

In chapter 15 of *PWR*, we discuss purity in terms of:
- Music
- TV and movies
- Video games
- Internet
- Social media

All of these have a great upside to them but also a dangerous downside if we are not the gate-keepers of what our kids are watching. Which of these items do you want to pay more attention to? **Ask God how He wants you to protect your children and write what He says below.**

LEGACY BUILDING EXERCISE

Take some time today to watch and listen alongside your kids. What are they watching? What are they hearing? Listen to the words, the attitudes, and the messages that are coming their way. In the same way, review what you're watching and listening to.

Make it a goal this week to sit down with your kids and repent for what you have allowed in your own life and what you have allowed in theirs. Explain that you want to be better at guarding their heart and that you can work on this together.

Remember, purity will require you to live differently, but you will never regret it. Not for a moment.

CHAPTER
16

TEACHING A WORK ETHIC

Fill in the blanks using Proverbs 12:24:
"The hand of the_____will _____but the slack hand will be put to forced labor." NASB

Rewrite Proverbs 12:24 in your own words and apply it to your own life. How is your work ethic and what do you model to your kids?

Now think of your kids. Are they hard workers? Do they finish what is before them? What is their attitude about school? If you feel good in those areas, let's go one step further. How aware are they of the needs around them? Do they initiate cleaning, taking out the trash, or returning something they borrowed in better condition than when they got it? Do your kids honor others by looking for ways to go above and beyond in helping?

Oftentimes, with so many things to work on, we can get overwhelmed. Pray through the different work ethic topics that are mentioned in this chapter.

Circle one that you want to work on with all your kids. Focus on that in this season.

School   Exercise   Chores

Jobs   Responsibility

LEGACY BUILDING EXERCISE

Have a conversation this week with your kids about their work ethic and the joy and satisfaction of hard work and seeing its benefits.

If you personally need to make a change, do it. Remember to always start with yourself. If you have not modeled a hard-working servant heart, repent and share how you are all going to make changes together.

CHAPTER
17

MONEY AND POSSESSIONS

 There are more than 800 references to money in the Bible. Below are three Scriptures that look at money from different angles.
Look them up and write out the one with which you most identify.

Psalm 16:5-6   *Philippians 4:11-13*   *1 Timothy 6:17-19*

Are you being a good steward of the money God has given you? Think through where most of it goes. If you don't currently have a budget, begin working to create one that is realistic for your family.

Jimmy and Laura shared several stories in *PWR* that began with urgent financial need and ended in miraculous provision. The steps they took each time looked something like this:

1) Pull the family together.
2) Share the problem.
3) Work hard and save, then give what you can.
4) Pray and believe in faith throughout the entire process.
5) Watch God provide.

Are you in a place of great need right now? If so, which of the steps mentioned above do you need to implement? We all want the "God provides" part to happen in our lives, but of the other steps, which one are you ready to begin doing with your family?

LEGACY BUILDING EXERCISE

Your kids watch and know you better than anyone else. No matter what you think about yourself, we suggest you go to each of your kids independently and ask them if they think you are a generous person. Do they see you tithing at church? Do they see you giving to the poor? Do they think that you value money and things over people?

Using some of the scriptures above, share with them the purpose of money and what it is meant to be used for. Don't forget to teach them that God blesses us so that we can bless others. Finish by asking them to pray with you on who you can bless with your resources.

CHAPTER
18

DEFINING MOMENTS

 Turn to *Matthew 3:13-17* and read the passage. Write out the words God spoke over Jesus. Why do you think God did that?

Now read Matthew 16:13-20. What did Jesus tell Peter in verses 18-19? **Write out what you would feel like if you heard God speak that over you.**

What particular defining moments are important to you and to your kids (birthdays, holiday traditions, turning 13, sweet 16, etc.)? *Prayerfully make a list and ask God if there are any other special moments He wants you to focus on as your children grow.*

LEGACY BUILDING EXERCISE

Make a plan to do something special in the next few months for each of your children. Capitalize on a special date coming up (birthday, graduation, etc.). Put thought into it so it will be something different and special to them. Ask a friend for ideas or to even come along with his or her kid and help. Make sure you make this about the kids. **Write your ideas below.**

CHAPTER
19

DATING AND ATTRACTION

We are made for attraction and desire, which play out in healthy friendships, dating, and marriage. So how do you handle such a sensitive topic with your children?

Where did you learn about sexuality? Circle your answer.
    Mom   Dad   Friends   TV/Movies   Other

"Watch over your heart with all diligence, for from it flow the springs of life."
Proverbs 4:23, NASB
"The plans of the diligent lead surely to advantage."
Proverbs 21:5, NASB

How do these Scriptures apply to intentional parenting and helping your child with this journey?

Your children will learn about sexuality from you and the world. Initiating conversations about the topic of sexuality creates space for open communication. It is best if we as the parents can lay the foundation for their understanding of sexuality. Then the things they hear elsewhere run through the filter that you have put in place.

What plan do you need for each of your children in each stage of their lives to ensure they learn about sexuality and relationships from you?

LEGACY BUILDING EXERCISE

Plan with your spouse to talk openly about attraction, desire, and sexuality with each of your kids. Start the dialogue earlier rather than later so that throughout their maturing process you can be the one they journey with.

If you need help knowing what is appropriate for your child's age/stage of development, or just advice on how to handle this important topic, talk with the children's ministry staff at your church, a pastor, or a trusted friend, or mentor, who has kids a few stages ahead of yours.

CHAPTER
20

FOCUSED AND INTENTIONAL

Three times a year we sit down with our kids and go through a simple exercise we call "Roles and Goals." Laura and the kids were not always excited about this, but now that our kids are grown, we see how God used it to keep us on track.

"So teach us to number our days, that we might present to You a heart of wisdom."
Psalm 90:12, NASB

What do you learn from this Scripture?

Read Ephesians 5:15-17 and write it out in your own words.

How should we live as a family in light of these Scriptures?

NOTES

LEGACY BUILDING EXERCISE

Sit down with each of your kids individually and explain the purpose and importance of Roles and Goals. **(The Roles and Goals worksheets are attached at the end of this workbook.). Help them think through and create what those goals are and write them on these worksheets. This is also a great opportunity for you to do the same for yourself. To keep the goals before you, post them on the wall in the bedroom or by the mirror in the bathroom.**

Check in once a month and see how everyone is doing! Again, take this one step at a time. This can be a difficult exercise for some personalities.

Remember, it is better to have two or three feasible goals than ten goals that you never actually have time to complete.

CHAPTER
21

WHERE DO WE GO FROM HERE?

Well, we end with what we all need—grace. We are all limited in our abilities, no matter how diligent and faithful we are.

God's grace is our continual place of strength, forgiveness, hope, and power.

 "But by the grace of God I am what I am, and His grace toward me did not prove vain, but I labored even more than all of them, yet not I, but the grace of God with me."
1 Corinthians 15:10, NASB

What do we learn about grace in this passage? How can grace strengthen and sustain us?

In the midst of the many things we have discussed and the many plans you have made regarding your family, make sure you remember to daily put on grace as you work with your kids and work on yourself. Consider how to give and speak grace to your children and to yourself despite your failures. Be faithful, be consistent, don't disengage when it gets hard, and *remember, parenting well occurs only by the grace of God.*

As we close, ask God for help; cry out to Him to parent you as you parent your kids! Ask Him for grace, wisdom, patience, love, and thank Him for forgiveness and redemption.

LEGACY BUILDING EXERCISE

Read the questions below and spend time with the Lord processing how to fully answer it and live in it. Once you have heard His answer, jot it down here or in a place you can easily find it.

How can I begin to fully receive God's grace in such a way that it actually makes an impact on my family?

What are ways I can be an example of godly grace to my children?

ROLES AND GOALS WORKSHEET

Spiritual
1.
2.
3.
4.

Physical
1.
2.
3.
4.

Mental
1.
2.
3.
4.

Social
1.
2.
3.
4.

Financial
1.
2.
3.
4.